DID a True Experience

Larry Berry

Presentation by *BookLeaf Publishing*

Web: www.bookleafpub.com

E-mail: info@bookleafpub.com

ISBN: 9789394788480

First edition 2022

DEDICATION

I dedicate this book to Peewee and Luke, my alters. You are just as important as I am.

ACKNOWLEDGEMENT

I'd like to thank my amazing partners, family, and friends that help support me every day and show us that we can be loved and cared for. I would like to give a special thank you to my Hierophant Nina Deckard for inspiring me, helping with edits, and finding me this opportunity. Finally, I'd like to thank Ashley Haney, my wife, my Little Fox, my rock, and the one that has helped me so much with getting me diagnosed, finding a therapist, and loving us through our bad days and good days.

DID

Dissociative life
Identity is not one
Disorder not broke

Little

My little plays in his forest
Running safe and free
He saved me from an evil
That I will never see.

He shines so brightly
So the world will never know
The true emotional pain
That he will never show.

Protector

My protector, strong and Proud
Promised to protect me from physical pain,
Watches over the door of my world.

I see the scars he tries to hide
Fighting against the pain
The only world he knew.

As we grow his world expands
No longer just pain
But finally, love reaches him.

Better

I am a better father
I am a better partner
I am a better friend
I am a better problem solver
I am a better problem starter
I am a better son
I am a better person with my DID

Trauma

Triggering the past
Reconciling with my alters
Accessing the memories
Utilizing therapy
Making the now
Accepting the future

We are multiple

We are multiple personalities trying our best not
to clash.
We are multiple planets trying not to smash
Smashing our planets would definitely cause a
clash
We are multiple personalities trying our best not
to smash

White Room

My room is so white and clean
So neat with no chaos to be seen
Yes they may have forest and beauty
They may have a fox that transforms into a cutie
But MY room
My room is white and clean I presume
I wonder if my white room will ever know
The true nature I wish I could show

Time

I used to miss time.
Day, weeks, even months
Because of you.
I hated you for that.
I hated that
I had to lose out on the only life I had.
I've learned that my missing time
Means you get to see your partners, your
children, your friends.
So yes,
I still don't like the missing time.
I love that you get to be happy
When I do.

Switch

I want to be productive and work hard
Switch
I just want to play
Switch
I just want you both to let me sleep

Switch
I want to buy a home and have a career
Switch
I want to flirt and have fun
Switch
I want us to be safe

Switch
I will follow the spirit and letter of the law to
make Order
Switch
I will follow the letter of the law and make
CHAOS
Switch
I will follow the Spirit of the law to keep us and
others Protected

Therapy

Therapy saved me.
Therapy made me face my demons and
turned them into friends.
Therapy showed me how
to love myself.
Therapy hit me so hard I fell
into different worlds where
different people lived and
man was that a lot.
Therapy taught me I am stronger than
I could have ever thought.

But therapy is hard.
Therapy has made me
cry for hours.
Therapy has made me
feel so small, so minuscule that
nothing I did could matter.
I am the host and therapy taught me
I would have to share my time.
Have to lose part of my life
at least for a time
so that we could grow and be trusted.
Therapy is worth it!

Vote

3 votes.
1 yes 1 no looks like we don't get to go.
1 yes 2 no looks like it's a no.
Yet when they're out. I don't get a vote or a say
3 votes are better than no control.

Fake it

AAAHH where am I?
When am I?
Fake it.
Be him until you can leave this place.
Anxiety rises
Palms sweat
Fake it
FAKE IT

Just silence

Sometimes silence is what I desire.
I hear of people sitting in silence
and I have always wondered what it truly meant.
I have sat and not made a sound,
but in my head,
the voices always come around.
Asking to come out, to play,
to solve that problem that won't go away.
There is always sound.
I just wish to have silence for one moment in my
life.
Just silence.

The job of a Fae

My job as Fae is to be so bright you can't see the
pain.
Be so friendly that no one can be mean to us
again.
I bring chaotic energy, not evil or bad.
Just the energy so don't be all mad.
I help you let loose and see the true joy of the
world.
Don't blame me when you get all swirled.
Swirled up in my cuteness or my bubbly ways.
You see I'm just chaotic in a truthful way.
As fae, we do not lie but we love to play.
To find loopholes in your words and add a little
fun in that way.

Howling at the moon

You hear me
howling
at the moon every night.
For they are the only one
that has truly listened to me over the years.

Through my pain.
When you were lost in that town
alone
is the first day I came to be.

I saw the moon and
howled into the night.
I saw a full moon and I truly knew
that they were going to be
the only one we could rely on
to help us sleep at night.

Partners

People that accept and love my alters
Affable to my alters even when there is conflict
Rejoice in my playful nature
Try to understand our DID the way I will try to
understand them
Neurodivergent in at least one way
Energizes me when I'm feeling low
Renders me speechless with the beauty they can
show
Sweet and loving to me when I disassociate

Disassociated

I…………………… am………….here…………
But……… not

What's your stuffie

What's your stuffie
Mine is a pooh
I've had since Two

What's your stuffie?
Does it have a name
Do you carry them around sometimes with no
shame?

What's your stuffie?
Do you have a lot
Or do you have one special one that just fills the
slot?

Toy Box

My box is where I keep all the toys.
But they don't play nice
in any way.
They cut,
they dig,
they try to overpower me
and get to Larry.
So I fight them back
day after day.
Working so hard so he never has to see
the toys in my box.
I've learned to smile through this kind of play
to find enjoyment
in the cutting and pain,
somehow.
I've gotten really good at keeping them at bay
and in their place.
The therapist wants me to
let Larry see them
and start to work on them as well.
But I'm afraid it would be a whole new level of
hell for him.

(Let it go)Trauma Holder

This is for my other trama holders out there.
From one to another.... Let go.
Let go of the memory that haunts you at night.
Let go of the pain that cut so deep
with no wound to be found.
Let go of the idea that without it you won't exist.
Let go of the notion that they can't handle the
memories or pain.
Maybe after writing this and telling you all to do
it.....
I can do the same.

It's okay (littles)

It's okay to be happy
It's okay to be fun
It's okay to want to play games
It's okay to talk to the therapist
It's okay to love
It's okay cry
It's okay to have snacks
It's okay to open up.